THE SPECTACULAR AND mostly TRUE ADVENTURES OF ANNIE KOPCHOVSKY

Amazing Annie

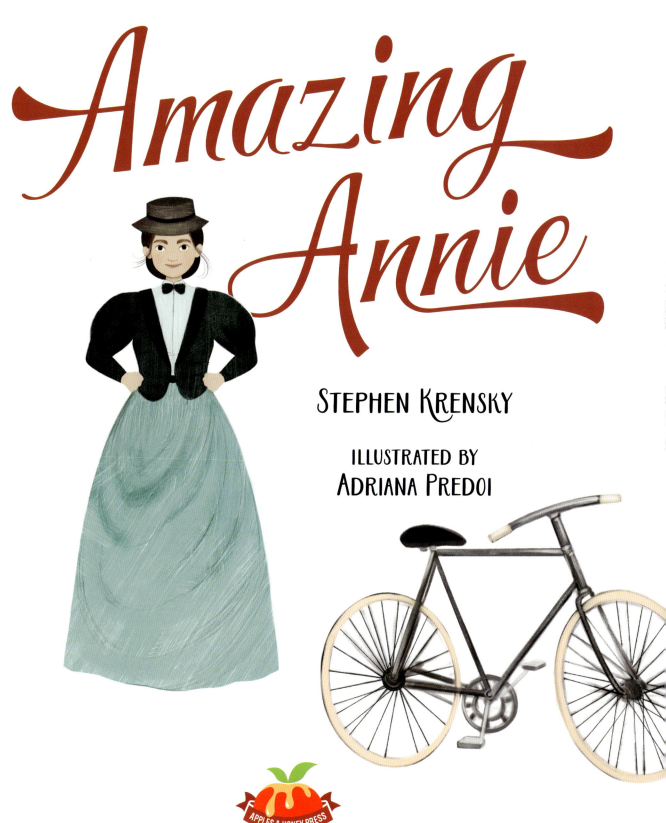

STEPHEN KRENSKY

ILLUSTRATED BY
ADRIANA PREDOI

APPLES & HONEY PRESS

For my granddaughter, who will soon have
her own amazing adventures. — S.K.

For Ana, my grandma. Now that I'm older,
I think of you more and more. — A.P.

The author wishes to acknowledge *Around the World on Two Wheels* by Peter Zheutlin, a comprehensive account of Annie Kopchovsky's trip.

The main text font is 19/24 Bicyclette Regular

Apples & Honey Press
An Imprint of Behrman House Publishers
Millburn, New Jersey 07041
www.applesandhoneypress.com

ISBN 978-1-68115-657-6

Text copyright © 2025 by Stephen Krensky
Illustrations copyright © 2025 by Behrman House

All rights reserved. No part of this publication may be translated, reproduced, stored in a retrieval system or transmitted, in any form or by any means, electronic, mechanical, photocopying, recording or otherwise, for any purpose, without express written permission from the publishers.

Library of Congress Cataloging-in-Publication Data

Names: Krensky, Stephen, author. | Predoi, Adriana, illustrator.
Title: Amazing Annie : the spectacular and mostly true adventures of Annie Kopchovsky / by Stephen Krensky ; illustrated by Adriana Predoi.
Description: Millburn, NJ : Apples & Honey Press, 2025. | Includes bibliographical references. | Audience: Ages 5-8. | Audience: Grades 2-3. | Summary: In the late 1800s, Annie Kopchosky sets out to achieve the unprecedented feat of biking around the world.
Identifiers: LCCN 2024020507 | ISBN 9781681156576 (hardcover)
Subjects: CYAC: Londonderry, Annie--Fiction. | Adventure and adventurers--Fiction. | Voyages around the world--Fiction. | Bicycles and bicycling--Fiction. | Jews--United States--Fiction. | United States--History--1865-1898--Fiction. | LCGFT: Biographical fiction. | Picture books.
Classification: LCC PZ7.K883 Am 2025 | DDC [E]--dc23
LC record available at https://lccn.loc.gov/2024020507

Design and art direction by Zach Marell
Edited by Dena Neusner
Printed in China

9 8 7 6 5 4 3 2 1

ANNIE KOPCHOVSKY was ready for a change. More than ready.

The year was 1894, and women weren't allowed to do very much besides get married and have children.

Annie had been born in Latvia. As a young girl, she had come to America with her family, a small drop in the great wave of Eastern European Jewish immigrants.

At first, life had seemed full of possibilities. But now her world felt small. She was tired of washing clothes, cooking meals, and cleaning the house.

She was also tired of her Boston neighbors treating her as an outsider just because she was Jewish.

Annie wanted some excitement. Some adventure. She hated being told what she shouldn't do just because she was a woman.

And then one day Annie had an idea about a recent invention—the bicycle.

It was a big idea.
It was a crazy idea.
A big and crazy idea.

"What I want," she decided, "is to be the first woman to ride a bicycle around the world."

Now when most people got an idea like that, they just stuck it in a drawer somewhere.

Not Annie. She might not become famous, but she was determined to show the world what a woman could do.

So, one day in June, Annie set off from downtown Boston. She had promised to go around the world in only fifteen months.

Unfortunately, Annie's bold hopes for a quick journey went downhill fast. Riding was hard, really hard, and she managed only eight to ten miles a day over bumpy dirt roads.

Even worse, Annie's skirt kept getting caught in the wheels. "Men don't have this problem," she observed. "They wear pants."

Women didn't wear pants. It was not appropriate. Not ladylike.

"That's silly," Annie told herself. "It makes sense to wear pants on a bicycle."

So she did.

Day after day, Annie and her new pants pedaled on. When she couldn't find a proper hotel to spend the night, Annie didn't worry.

She slept in barns . . .

or under bridges . . .

In November, Annie boarded a ship in New York City headed to France. During the long ocean voyage, she talked a lot about her adventures. It was fun to be the center of attention.

"There was one time," she said, "when I fell off my bicycle on a train track."

"Did it hurt?" asked a little girl.

"Not a bit," said Annie. "But then I heard a train coming. . . ." Annie exhaled deeply. "It roared right by on the next track. Almost flattened me like a pancake."

That was a close call—or it would have been, except that it wasn't true.

The truth was that Annie had discovered how much people loved hearing her stories. And she loved inventing the stories they wanted to hear.

In France, Annie rode past ancient castles and modern grape vineyards. There were outdoor markets selling fruits and vegetables.

One day, three masked men jumped out from the bushes. They grabbed her bicycle and threw her to the ground.

As Annie stood up, she faced the robbers squarely.

"You seem to have mistaken me for a helpless woman," she told them. "I assure you I am not. And I am not a wealthy woman, either."

When the robbers found only a few coins inside her purse, they threw them back at her and melted away into the gloom.

From southern France, Annie sailed next for the Near East.

As a Jewish woman she was excited about a quick visit to Jerusalem. The city was part of so many prayers and traditions. Here was the Western Wall, the center of Jewish life in Biblical times.

She could actually touch it.

Then came Singapore.

And Shanghai.

Sometimes she got lost or tired.
But she still had a long way to go.

So, she pedaled on.

When Annie wasn't riding, she stayed busy dreaming up tales to tell. Crowds filled theaters and ballrooms to hear her stories—even when they were made up!

"I'll never forget hunting Bengal tigers in the jungle," she told more than one audience. "They growl fiercely—but only just before they're about to pounce," she added.

"Another time I was crossing a frozen river in China—and I fell right through the ice! In that moment I felt like the world's biggest icicle."

In March, Annie returned to America by ship from Japan. But she wasn't done yet. She still had to ride across the entire country to get home by September.

She was slowed up a bit, though, when she collided with a runaway horse and wagon on the road to Los Angeles.

"I escaped," Annie told a large audience that night, "with a black eye, a scarred face, and a bruised body for my trouble."

Onward she went through Arizona, New Mexico, and Texas. The desert landscape was so different from the jungles of India or the rice paddies of Japan.

In El Paso, Annie was treated like royalty. A local bicycle club escorted her into town, and she was honored at a big party in a fancy hotel.

Finally, more than fourteen months after starting out, Annie returned to Boston. She was home at last!

Her family was proud of her achievements. But most of all, they were happy to have their amazing Annie back in one piece.

Annie's trip was big news. It was exciting to see her name and picture in newspapers both near and far. In fact, the *New York World* declared her trip to be "the most extraordinary journey ever undertaken by a woman."

Annie could not have said it better herself.

The  World.

ANNIE COHEN KOPCHOVSKY (1870-1947) was born into a world where women had few choices for creating independent lives. In nineteenth-century America, many women were discouraged from having jobs outside the home, and they weren't even allowed to vote. Annie was determined to do better for herself, but it wasn't easy.

Annie sold buttons and photographs and gave speeches as she traveled, to earn money for the trip. In addition, the Londonderry Lithia Spring Water Company of New Hampshire agreed to help pay her expenses if she would change her name to Annie Londonderry—so she did.

But Annie had another reason for using a fake name. Her real name was clearly a Jewish name, and there were many places where people were prejudiced against Jewish people. Annie felt safer keeping her Jewish identity hidden during her trip.

Unlike some of the stories she told, Annie was very much a real person. After returning to her family, she later worked as a journalist, saleswoman, and businesswoman. Annie lived for another fifty years, but rarely rode a bicycle again.

As for how history might finally judge her accomplishments, Annie was not worried. She later declared, "I am 'a new woman' if that term means that I believe I can do anything that any man can do."

Annie Londonderry, circa 1896, Studio Tourne